Hanukkah Lights, Hanukkah Nights

by Leslie Kimmelman

illustrated by John Himmelman

HarperCollins*Publishers*

Hanukkah Lights, Hanukkah Nights
Text copyright © 1992 by Leslie A. Kimmelman
Illustrations copyright © 1992 by John Himmelman
Printed in the U.S.A. All rights reserved.
2   3   4   5   6   7   8   9   10

Library of Congress Cataloging-in-Publication Data
Kimmelman, Leslie.
   Hanukkah lights, Hanukkah nights / by Leslie Kimmelman ; illustrated by
John Himmelman.
      p.   cm.
   Summary: An extended family celebrates the eight nights of Hanukkah.
   ISBN 0-06-020368-4. — ISBN 0-06-020369-2 (lib. bdg.)
   1. Hanukkah—Juvenile literature. [1. Hanukkah.]
I. Himmelman, John, ill.   II. Title
BM695.H3K56   1992   91-15633
296.4' 35—dc20   CIP
[E]   AC

For Natalie and Greg,
two bright lights in my life

My relatives come from far and wide

to help us celebrate Hanukkah.

My family lights the shammash candle.
Tonight is the first night of Hanukkah.

My grandmothers sip the chicken soup.
Tonight is the second night of Hanukkah.

My aunts chant the holiday blessings.
Tonight is the third night of Hanukkah.

The nieces spin their four-sided dreidels.
Tonight is the fourth night of Hanukkah.

The nephews fight like Maccabees.
Tonight is the fifth night of Hanukkah.

My uncles flip potato latkes.

Tonight is the sixth night of Hanukkah.

Our kittens play with chocolate gelt.
Tonight is the seventh night of Hanukkah.

The cousins sing the holiday songs.
Tonight is the eighth night of Hanukkah.

All the candles are shining brightly.
Happy, happy Hanukkah!

HANUKKAH, THE FESTIVAL OF LIGHTS

Every winter, for eight days and nights, Jewish people all over the world celebrate the holiday of Hanukkah. With the *shammash*, or leader, candle, they light the *menorah*. Songs are sung; potato pancakes called *latkes* are eaten; *dreidels* are spun. Sometimes money—*gelt*—or gifts are given.

But the real story of Hanukkah happened long ago.

More than two thousand years ago in Syria, there lived a king named Antiochus. He wanted everyone to pray only to his gods, so he ordered the Jewish people to stop practicing their religion or face terrible punishment. Some Jews were afraid, and they obeyed the king. But Mattathias Maccabee and his five sons refused to pray to Antiochus's gods. The five Maccabee brothers fought King Antiochus. Many other Jews fought with them.

After three long years, the Maccabees won.

Once again, the Jews were free to pray in their temple in Jerusalem. But inside the temple, everything was smashed and broken. Worst of all, the Eternal Light, which burned day and night, had gone out. The Jews looked everywhere and finally found enough oil to burn the lamp for one day. Then came the miracle: When the lamp was lit, the oil burned for *eight* days and *eight* nights.

Today at Hanukkah, Jewish people remember the Maccabees' victory, and the freedom they won to pray to their own God. By lighting the menorah eight times, Jewish people remember the miracle of one day's oil lasting for eight days and nights. When latkes are made at Hanukkah, they are fried in oil as a reminder. And when the dreidel is spun round, the letters on its sides say NES GADOL HAYAH SHEM: "A great miracle happened there."